THE SUBTLE ART OF NOT GIVING UP

45 Capsules of Motivation for When You're Tired, Stuck, or Starting Over

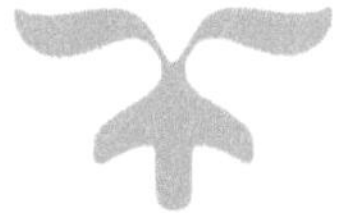

BY

ANKIT SHARMA

Copyright @ 2025 NERDSTABLE

www.nerdschool.online

Table of Contents

Foreword

"It was the best of times, it was the worst of times..." — *Charles Dickens, A Tale of Two Cities*

It always begins like that, doesn't it?

The contrast.
The tension between light and shadow.
Between holding it all together—and slowly falling apart.

Because life rarely arrives in one clean emotion.
It's grief and laughter in the same breath.
Hope and hopelessness sharing the same room.
Strength held up by trembling hands.

Maybe that's why we remember lines like that.
Because *they feel like us.*

"It was a bright cold day in April, and the clocks were striking thirteen."
— George Orwell, 1984

You've felt that kind of day too, haven't you?

Where the world looks normal—maybe even beautiful—
but **something underneath is off**.
You're dressed. You're working. You're smiling.
But inside, the hour feels wrong. The weight feels off.

Like your internal clock is ticking in a language no one else hears.

This book isn't written for the days when you feel powerful.
It's written for the mornings when you wake up, and your mind says,
"I can't do this again."
But you still get up.

Not because you're okay.
But because **you've decided to keep showing up**—even in pieces.

That's not weakness.
That's *unseen strength*.

"In a hole in the ground there lived a hobbit."
— *J.R.R. Tolkien, The Hobbit*

No great journey ever began with fanfare.
Sometimes, it starts in a hole.
In discomfort. In ordinary places.
In doubt, or resistance, or messy middle-of-nowhere moments.

But eventually, something stirs.
A whisper. A pull. A quiet rebellion inside you that says:
"There has to be more than this."

And so you go—
Not toward some heroic destiny,
but toward **your own quiet unfolding**.

That's what this book is.
A companion for the in-between.
For the days before the triumph.
For the times when you're not slaying dragons—just trying
to eat, breathe, and not quit.

---

*"It is a truth universally
acknowledged..."*
— Jane Austen, Pride and Prejudice

Yes, we've all been fed truths like that.
Universal ideas about what success looks like.
What strength looks like.
What healing should feel like.

But here's another truth:
Healing rarely looks poetic.

It's not always yoga mats and sunsets.
Sometimes, healing looks like brushing your teeth when
you don't want to exist.
Sometimes, it looks like texting a friend "I'm okay" when
you're lying through your teeth—
because you're just not ready to explain how much it hurts.

This book won't judge you for that.
It won't ask you to "be positive."
It will ask you to **be real**.

---

*"As Gregor Samsa awoke one morning
from uneasy dreams he found himself
transformed in his bed into a gigantic*

insect."
— Franz Kafka, The Metamorphosis

Haven't we all woken up like Gregor, at least once?

Not in our bodies—but in our minds.
Feeling unfamiliar to ourselves.
Alien in our own skin.
Wondering how we got here.
Feeling like life has made us something... *else.*

But unlike Gregor, you're still changing.
Still moving.
Still not done yet.

And this book?
It's not the solution.
It's not a transformation plan.

It's a **hand on your back**,
a **lamp in your cave**,
a **matchstick on a cold night** that whispers:

"Fall apart. But don't stay there. You still have more becoming left to do."

"Once upon a time and a very good time
it was there was a moocow coming
down along the road..."
— James Joyce, A Portrait of the Artist
as a Young Man

Even brilliance begins with confusion.
Even the artist begins as a child, trying to make sense of a world too big, too fast, too strange.

And maybe that's you right now.

Trying to make meaning of the mess.
Trying to be the artist of your own life story.
Even when the canvas feels too empty.
Or too cluttered with the past.

This book won't give you all the answers.
But it will help you ask better questions.
It will help you slow down enough to remember that you are not a machine.
You are a soul in motion.
And motion—**even messy, painful motion**—is proof that you are still alive.

The Subtle Art of Not Giving Up is not a self-help book in the traditional sense.
It's a survival book.
A permission slip.
A breadcrumb trail back to yourself.

It contains no steps to success,
but it *will* help you get through your worst day with a little more grace.

Inside these pages are 45 Capsules—part story, part mirror, part medicine.
They're meant to be taken one at a time.
Not consumed, but absorbed.
Not devoured, but digested slowly—like words you whisper to yourself when no one's watching.

Each capsule is a moment.
A door.
A decision to keep going, *not perfectly—but presently.*

So if you're tired,
if you're lost,
if you're trying to build a life out of pieces—

Then welcome.
You're in the right place.
You don't have to fall apart alone.

You're not weak for breaking.
You're powerful for beginning again.

And this book?
It won't save you.
But it will *sit beside you while you save yourself.*

– Ankit Sharma
(Author and Mentor)

THE SUBTLE ART OF NOT GIVING UP

CAPSULE 1

The Bamboo Tree

"...it's all building your foundation."

In a quiet village surrounded by misty hills and thick forests, a humble farmer did something curious.
He cleared a small patch of land, dug a shallow hole, and gently planted a **bamboo seed**.

Every morning, without fail, he watered it.
Every week, he cleared weeds from around it.
Every month, he checked the soil.
And every year... he waited.

But the bamboo did not grow.

One year passed. Nothing.
Two years passed. Nothing.
Three years. Still nothing.
Four years. Not even a bud.

His neighbours laughed.
His friends pitied him.
Even his family asked, "Why waste your time on something that gives you nothing back?"

But the farmer had read about the bamboo.
He knew something they didn't.

Then, in the **fifth year**, something remarkable happened.

The bamboo finally **broke through the soil**.
And within just **six weeks**, it shot up to **over 80 feet tall**.

What was it doing all those years?

It was not sleeping. It was **working beneath the surface**. Its roots were spreading wide and deep, preparing to hold the weight of greatness.

If it had grown any earlier, it would have collapsed. But now, it was **unshakable.**

Lessons in the Quiet

Your journey to crack UGC NET might feel the same.

You're studying. You're revising. You're solving questions.
And sometimes, it feels like… nothing is changing.
Your marks aren't improving. Your memory isn't sharp. You feel stuck.

But remember the bamboo.

Every hour you put in…
Every mock test you take…
Every topic you revise…

…it's all **building your foundation**.

You are not behind.
You are not stuck.
You are growing.

And when the time comes—**you will rise faster than you ever imagined.**

Daily Action:

> ➢ Write down **3 things you've done today** that strengthened your roots.

> ➢ Remind yourself and say this aloud: **"I am growing roots. I will rise when it's time."**

CAPSULE 2

The Pen That Moves Mountains

"A goal unwritten is just a wish."

Imagine this.

There are two people standing in front of the same whiteboard.

Both have dreams.
Both have ambition.
Both say, "This is what I want to achieve."

But only one of them picks up a marker... and writes it down.

Which one is more likely to actually make it?

A study from **Dominican University** decided to find out.

Researchers took two groups of people:

> One group simply thought about their goals.
> The other group **wrote their goals down**.

The result?

The group that wrote down their goals was **42% more likely to achieve them**.

That's not magic. That's psychology.

Writing down your goals forces your brain to take them seriously.
It creates clarity. It makes you accountable. It shifts a dream from fantasy to form.

> ➢ Suddenly, it's real.
> ➢ You've declared it.
> ➢ You've committed to it.

Lessons in the Quiet

Now think about your UGC NET journey.

Have you written your goals down?

Have you **declared** what you want?
Do you know **how many questions you want to get right?**
Do you know **what books you'll complete and by when?**
Or is everything still floating in your mind, hazy and unspoken?

Start small.
One goal. One line. One written statement.

That single action alone could make you **42% more likely to succeed.**

The best part? It doesn't matter how or where you write it.

> ➤ Use a notebook.
> ➤ Use Google Docs (I call mine **"Goalkeeper"**)
> ➤ Or write it in your planner right now.

Some people write **yearly goals**.

I prefer **quarterly quests**—3 months, 3 focused targets.
No more than 3 or 4 goals at a time.
Why? Because when everything is a priority, nothing is.

Daily Action:

> ➤ Write down 3 clear goals for the next 30 days.
> ➤ Make them visible. Stick them on your wall, your notebook, or your phone screen.

What you write becomes what you work toward.

"And every great journey begins with a sentence."

CAPSULE 3

The Infinite To-Do List

"You'll never finish it all—and that's okay."

Have you ever ended a day feeling like you were sprinting the whole time…
but barely moved an inch?

Your **to-do list is longer** at night than it was in the morning.
Your mind is running laps, and yet your goals feel just as far away.

You think:
"If I just wake up earlier… work a bit harder… push through the weekend… maybe then I'll finally catch up."

But here's the truth:
You won't.
And **you're not supposed to.**

In his powerful book *4,000 Weeks*, author Oliver Burkeman lays it out simply:
We only get around **4,000 weeks in our lifetime**. That's it.
And our to-do list?
It's **infinite.**

You will always have more emails to answer, more books to read, more people to help, more things to learn.
You will never "finish" everything.

At first, that might sound depressing.
But it's not.

It's freeing.

Because once you accept you can't do it all—you're finally allowed to choose **what truly matters**.

Lessons in the Quiet

You don't have to conquer the entire mountain.
Just **pick the peak that matters most** and climb that one with everything you've got.

You don't need to be amazing at everything.
You need to be deeply focused on **what moves your life forward**.

In your UGC NET journey, this means:

> ➢ You don't need to study 12 hours a day.
> ➢ You don't need to cover 10 mock tests in a week.
> ➢ You don't need to read every book ever written.

You just need to do **the most important things consistently**.

> ➢ Prioritize **understanding**, not rushing.
> ➢ Prioritize **mock tests**, not mindless hours.
> ➢ Prioritize **progress**, not perfection.

Some areas of your life will be mediocre—and that's okay.
Let them be.
Focus on your mission.

Daily Action:

> ➢ Look at your current to-do list.
> ➢ Circle the **3 most important items** that will move your goal forward.
> ➢ Leave the rest for later (or not at all).

"You weren't born to finish everything.
*You were born to **finish what matters**."*

CAPSULE 4

Revisit to Reinforce

"Goals remembered are goals revived."

Most people never achieve their goals for one simple reason:

They **forget** them.

> ➤ Mistake 1: They never set goals in the first place.
> ➤ Mistake 2: If they do set goals, they don't write them down.
> ➤ Mistake 3: If they write them down, they **never look at them again.**

Think about it.

You set goals in January. You're fired up.
By February, they're buried under work, errands, classes, and deadlines.
By March, you don't even remember what those goals were.

It's not because you're lazy.
It's because you're **busy being human.**

But here's a secret almost no one talks about:
You don't need more goals.
You just need to **revisit the ones you already set.**

One glance a week.
One moment a day.

That's all it takes.

Some of the most consistent high performers have a **tiny ritual**:

- ➢ Once a week, they review their goals.
- ➢ Every morning, they check their top priorities.
- ➢ They **reset, refocus, and realign**.

Lessons in the Quiet

I call mine a **Weekly Reset** and a **Morning Manifesto**.

Every Sunday, I ask:
"What were my quarterly quests? How are they going?"

Every morning, I ask:
"What are my top 3 priorities for today?"

It takes less than a minute.
But that minute is a **needle-mover**.
Because it stops me from drifting into distraction.
It pulls me back to the **mission I chose**.

You don't need a perfect system.
You just need a **ritual of remembering**.

- ➢ Tape your goals to the wall.
- ➢ Set a calendar reminder every Sunday evening.
- ➢ Stick a post-it on your desk with your top 3 priorities.

Whatever keeps them in sight, keeps them **in action**.

And if you fall off for a few days? Or weeks?

Welcome to the club.
We all do.

What matters is not that you forgot—
What matters is that you **come back**.

Daily Action:

- ➢ Review your weekly goals in the morning for 10 seconds.

➢ On Sundays, reflect: "What moved forward this week?"

"Goals don't work unless you do. But more importantly—Goals don't work unless you remember them."

CAPSULE 5

The Phone Fast

"Control your mornings, control your mind."

We all do it.

We wake up, reach for our phone…
…and before we even realize it, we're lost in a whirlwind of WhatsApp messages, Instagram reels, emails, and endless scrolling.

That first hour of your day?
Hijacked.

Your mind was fresh. Clear. Ready to take on the day.
But instead of planning your goals, you got sucked into someone else's world.

Here's what researchers are discovering now:
One of the most powerful things you can do to **protect your motivation** and **regain focus** is a habit called:

Phone Fasting.

It's simple.
But not easy.

- ➢ **No phone for the first 15 minutes after waking up.**
- ➢ **No phone during the last 60 minutes before sleep.**

Instead of scrolling, start doing:
Brush your teeth.
Splash cold water.

Make your bed.
Read one page.
Go for a short walk.

This early momentum **shifts your dopamine direction**—
from distraction to discipline.

And at night?
Power down.
Put your phone in another room.
Let your brain breathe.

"You don't need to fight the phone all day.
Just take back the first and last chapter of your story."

Lessons in the Quiet

Your phone is not evil.
But it is designed to **steal your attention**.
And if you don't manage it—it will manage your life.

The goal isn't to never use your phone.
The goal is to **reclaim your mental space**.

In the morning, your brain is at its sharpest.
It's searching for direction.
Give it **purpose**, not notifications.

At night, your brain is trying to **wind down**.
Don't blast it with more dopamine.
Give it silence. Stillness. Rest.

Students who adopt **phone fasting** report:

> - More focused study blocks
> - Less brain fog
> - Higher motivation
> - Better sleep
> - A calmer mind

You don't need 5 hours of discipline.
Start with **15 minutes in the morning.**
60 minutes at night.

That's where motivation hides.
Not in apps.
But in awareness.

Daily Action:

> - Set a timer: 15 minutes phone-free after waking up.
> - Create a phone-free zone 1 hour before sleep.

➢ Notice how your **energy shifts**.

CAPSULE 6

Systems Over Struggle

"Success doesn't need intensity. It needs intention."

Let's be honest.
Motivation isn't always the problem.
Often, it's that we don't know **what to do next.**

Think about going to the gym without a workout plan.
You stand there awkwardly, unsure where to start… and
end up walking out.
But if you walk in with a list:

> ➤ 5 min warm-up
> ➤ 3 sets squats
> ➤ 2 rounds pushups

—you just follow the script.

That's the difference between **planning** and **doing**.
Planning removes decision fatigue. It makes action
automatic.

Now let's talk about getting better at something.

Want to be a better writer? Write 100 pages.
Want to be great at YouTube? Post 100 videos.
Want to teach better? Record 100 lessons.

Quantity turns into quality—**as long as you keep going.**

And one more thing:

Exercise in the morning is like fuel.
Even a 15-minute walk outdoors resets your brain.

It's not about the calories.
It's about the clarity.
You return with more focus, more light, more drive.

But even with all of this… life can still get messy.
That's why you need **defaults**.

"If it's 5 PM, I go to the gym."
"If I have 30 minutes free, I revise 10 questions."
"No decision. No debate. Just default."

Lessons in the Quiet

If you want to stop procrastinating, don't just force action. **Design your system.**

- ➤ Plan your day the night before.
- ➤ Build consistency with small reps.
- ➤ Exercise in the morning—body moves, brain wakes up.
- ➤ Set defaults for what you'll do when your time frees up.

That's how you eliminate friction.
That's how you build a life of momentum.

Because motivation is like a spark.
It gets things started.
But systems?
They keep the fire burning.

Start planning before doing.
Start repeating before perfecting.
Start moving before overthinking.

Daily Action:

- ➤ Write down your "default habits" for morning, evening, and breaks.
- ➤ Plan your next day's top 3 tasks before sleeping.
- ➤ Take a 10-minute walk before your first study session.

CAPSULE 7

The Halo Effect

"First impressions are powerful. But not always accurate."

Imagine this.

You walk into a classroom, and someone sits across from you—well-dressed, confident posture, warm smile. Instantly, your mind makes a decision:

They must be smart.
They must be friendly.
They must be doing well in life.

But you've never spoken to them.
You don't know their name.
You have zero evidence.

This is called the **Halo Effect**—a psychological bias where **one visible trait** influences our judgment of everything else about a person.

> ➤ If someone is physically attractive, we assume they're intelligent or kind.
> ➤ If someone speaks fluently, we think they must be a great leader.
> ➤ If someone dresses poorly, we might assume they're lazy or careless.

And it's not just in classrooms or friend circles.

A teacher may believe a student who excels in math is great at all subjects.

A politician who's charismatic might be assumed to be a capable leader—even before they've made a single policy.

We all fall for it—every day.
And the scary part?
It also works in **reverse.**

One visible flaw—messy hair, bad handwriting, low marks in one test—and we start believing **a whole story** that might not even be true.

Lessons in the Quiet

You can't erase the Halo Effect.
But you can learn to **use it wisely.**

For yourself:

> ➢ Make a strong first impression—dress with intention, speak clearly, and lead with a smile.
> ➢ Show up prepared. That alone can shift how people treat you.

For others:

> ➢ Pause before judging.
> ➢ Ask: *"Do I know this person beyond what I see right now?"*
> ➢ Recognize when your mind is filling in the blanks unfairly.

In your UGC NET journey, this matters more than you think:

You might feel discouraged by **one subject you struggle with**, assuming you're not smart enough overall. That's the reverse halo.
Remember: **You are not your weakest score.**
You're a work in progress—with layers.

Pro Tip: Start your preparation with the **easiest subject or unit**. When you do well in it, you create a **positive momentum**. This becomes your **own Halo Effect—** helping you believe you're capable across the board.

That early success shapes your confidence in every other subject.

And one positive habit—like showing up on time, keeping your workspace neat, or helping a peer—can create a **positive halo** that carries over into how others (and you) view your entire identity.

Daily Action:

> ➢ Be intentional with your first impressions—online and offline.
> ➢ Identify one person you've unfairly judged based on a single trait—and try to see them more fully.
> ➢ Repeat to yourself: **"One trait doesn't define the whole person—including me."**

CAPSULE 8

The Odyssey Plan

"You have more paths than you think."

We grow up thinking life follows a straight line.

You study hard.
You choose a subject.
You get a job in that field.
And that's it.

But what if that path… isn't the one you truly want?

Back in 2019, a young programmer stumbled upon an idea from Stanford professors **Bill Burnett and Dave Evans**. It was called the **Odyssey Plan**—a life-design exercise that asks you to explore **three possible futures.**

1. **What does your life look like in 5 years if you continue down your current path?**
2. **What does it look like if you took a completely different path?**
3. **And what does it look like if you took a wildly different path where money, expectations, and opinions didn't matter at all?**

Sounds simple. But this experiment changes everything.

Because when you answer these three questions honestly, something magical happens:

You realize how **many more lives you could live**.
You see how big your world actually is.

And suddenly, that one fixed track you've been on?
It becomes **just one option**—not the only one.

Lessons in the Quiet

Most people build their lives around what they studied, what their parents expect, or what they're *"supposed to do."*
But you? You have choices.
You can **design** your life—not just drift through it.

Try this today.

Take out a notebook and write down your three answers.

1. Path 1: Where does your current route take you in five years?
2. Path 2: What if you changed direction entirely different field, city, or purpose?
3. Path 3: What if you lived *without* fear—no concern for money, judgment, or tradition?

You might be surprised by how exciting and possible these other futures are.

Even if you don't act on them right away, just **knowing they exist** gives you power.
It gives you perspective.
It gives you permission to be **more than one thing.**

Daily Action:

- ➤ Do the Odyssey Plan. Write three five-year visions of your life.
- ➤ Compare them. Which one feels the most alive?
- ➤ Remind yourself: **You are not stuck. You are designing.**

CAPSULE 9

Track It Like a Game

"Progress feels like power. Use it."

Have you ever noticed how **video games** can keep kids (and adults) glued to a screen for hours?

Even kids with short attention spans will sit for *three, four, five* hours—completely focused, fully immersed.

So... what's the secret?

It's not just flashy graphics.
It's not just explosions and music.
It's **progress.**

Game designers are experts at feeding us **small wins**:

> ➢ XP bars that slowly fill up
> ➢ Coins and rewards for completing tasks
> ➢ "Level Up!" animations with sound effects
> ➢ New gear, new powers, new maps
> ➢ A clear path of what's next

And when you see yourself progressing—even by **just 1%**—you want to keep going.

"Progress is addicting."

Lessons in the Quiet

Here's the thing:
Motivation dies when you don't see movement.

But the moment you track your progress—even in the simplest way—you light the fire again.

> ➤ Cross off each topic you complete.
> ➤ Tick your daily study boxes in the planner.
> ➤ Record your mock test scores and watch them rise.
> ➤ Create your own XP bar: 0/100 topics done → 100/100.
> ➤ Celebrate milestones like levels—"Volume 1 Complete!" "Mock Test 5 Mastered!"

Your brain loves progress.
So give it **evidence** that you're moving forward.

Make your preparation feel like a game.
Reward yourself.
Track your moves.
Watch the bars fill.

This isn't just about fun—it's about **tricking your brain into wanting to come back tomorrow.**

Daily Action:

> ➤ Create a simple tracker (table, calendar, checklist).
> ➤ Check off one win every single day.
> ➤ Every time you check a box, tell yourself: **"I'm levelling up."**

CAPSULE 10

The Batman Effect

"When in doubt—be someone braver."

When Adele first started performing live, she had a problem.

She was terrified.
Her voice was world-class. Her songs were pure emotion.
But getting on stage? That fear almost stopped her.

So what did she do?

She created someone else.
She imagined herself as a different person—a fearless, powerful alter ego.
She called her **Sasha Carter**—a blend of two singers she admired deeply.

And when she stepped onto the stage, it wasn't Adele anymore.
It was **Sasha Carter**.

Sasha was bold. Sasha owned the spotlight.
Sasha didn't tremble—she performed.

This mental trick gave Adele the courage to keep going, even when the real her was filled with doubt.

And science backs this up.

In a famous study, researchers split kids into groups and asked them to complete problem-solving tasks.

But here's the twist:
Some kids were told to imagine they were **Batman** or
Dora the Explorer while doing the task.

Guess what?

Those kids:

> ➤ **Performed better**
> ➤ **Stuck with the challenge longer**
> ➤ **Enjoyed the task more**

Why?
Because they weren't held back by their regular fears.
They were channelling a version of themselves that was
bigger and braver.

Lessons in the Quiet

We all have moments where fear creeps in.

- ➤ You sit in front of a mock test and freeze.
- ➤ You're about to start a hard topic and feel overwhelmed.
- ➤ You compare yourself to others and suddenly doubt everything.

That's when the **Batman Effect** comes in.

You step out of yourself—and into someone else.

- ➤ Be the "Scholar Version" of you.
- ➤ Be the "UGC NET Champion" version of you.
- ➤ Be the "Teacher" version who explains the topic confidently.

You don't have to be perfect.
You just have to **borrow the courage** from the version of you that already exists inside.

This isn't fake.
It's focused imagination.
And sometimes, your mind just needs permission to perform.

Daily Action:

- ➤ Create your alter ego. Give them a name and attitude.
- ➤ The next time you feel nervous or unmotivated, ask:
  "What would *they* do right now?"
- ➤ Channel that version of you—especially during tests, revision, and teaching.

CAPSULE 11

Later is a Lie

"The right time isn't coming. You are."

There's something you've been putting off.
You know exactly what it is.

- Starting that side project
- Launching a YouTube channel
- Messaging that friend you keep meaning to reconnect with
- Organizing your study plan
- Taking your goal—UGC NET, your career, your life—seriously

It's been sitting quietly in the back of your mind.
Waiting.
You tell yourself, *"Not now. Later."*

Maybe when things calm down.
Maybe next month.
Maybe when you're less tired, more confident, less overwhelmed.

But here's the truth you already know:

Later is a lie.

Your life won't magically become less busy.
Six weeks from now will feel just like today.
Your brain will find another reason, another delay, another excuse.

And the task will still be there.
Waiting.
Quietly collecting dust.

Until one day, you look back and wonder:
Why didn't I start sooner?

Later is a disease that will take all of your dreams and goals and ambitions to the grave.

Lessons in the Quiet

What we often forget is: **the hard part isn't doing the thing—it's starting.**

Once you start, the weight lifts.
The fear shrinks.
The clarity appears.

This is not about hustling harder.
It's about being **honest** with yourself.

You're not saying, *"I'll never do this."*
You're saying *"I'll do it later."*
But **later is the graveyard of all your unlived dreams.**

So instead of waiting for confidence—act.
Instead of waiting for clarity—start.
Instead of waiting for the perfect day—make today good enough.

This capsule?
It's not just for you.
It's a note to myself too.

I need to keep reminding myself:
"Start now, or carry regret later."

Daily Action:

> ➤ Write down ONE thing you've been putting off for weeks.
> ➤ Take **any step** toward it today—send the message, open the file, create the folder.
> ➤ Remind yourself: **"I don't need the right time. I just need to begin."**

CAPSULE 12

Pottery Class Paradox

"Perfection comes from practice, not pause."

There was a pottery class.

The teacher did something unusual:
She split her students into **two groups**.

Group 1 was told:
*"You only need to make **one pot**—but it must be perfect."*
They had the **entire semester** to craft that single pot.

Group 2 was told:
*"Make **as many pots** as you can. Don't worry about quality—just make more."*

At the end of the semester, they judged the results.

And here's the surprise:

The **best pots**—the most creative, the most balanced, the most beautiful—came from **Group 2.**

Why?

Because while Group 1 was **overthinking**, tweaking
endlessly, stuck in fear...
Group 2 was **making**.
They were failing fast.
Fixing.
Improving.
Learning by doing.

And in the process, they got better. Much better.

Lessons in the Quiet

This is how most people approach their goals:
They wait.
They overprepare.
They chase perfection.

But what they really need is: **more reps.**

Want to become a better writer? Write 50 pages.
Want to become a better teacher? Record 50 classes.
Want to crack UGC NET Paper I? Solve 500 questions.

Every attempt teaches you more than any plan ever will.
Mistakes are not setbacks—they're stepping stones.

You don't need a **perfect study plan**.
You need a **habit of showing up**.

> - Stop obsessing over the perfect notes.
> - Stop rewriting the same topic over and over.
> - Start completing chapters. Start solving mocks.

Start making **your pots**.

The more you make, the better you become.
Quantity creates quality.
That's the paradox—and the power—of practice.

Daily Action:

> - Choose progress over perfection today.
> - Set a small, repeatable goal: "Solve 10 questions," "Revise 1 topic," or "Write 1-page notes."
> - Repeat. Daily. Let quantity build your mastery.

CAPSULE 13

Parable of the Boat

"You can't be angry at an empty boat."

On a foggy morning, a man was rowing his boat peacefully down a river.

Suddenly—**BANG!**
Another boat crashed into his.

He was furious.
He stood up, shouted into the mist, ready to confront the careless person who hit him.

But when the fog cleared...
he saw the boat was **empty**.

No one inside.
It had broken loose from a dock and simply **drifted into him**.

And just like that, his anger melted away.
Because you can't be mad at an empty boat.
There was **no intention** to harm him. Just an accident. A coincidence.

And that's the point.

Lessons in the Quiet

Life will bump into you.

Someone will forget to reply.
Someone will snap at you in traffic.
Someone will say something harsh or miss a deadline or seem careless.

And your instinct might be to get **angry**—to assume it's personal.

But pause.

Ask yourself:
"Is this just an empty boat?"

Most people aren't trying to hurt you.
They're not plotting against you.
They're just drifting through their own fog—dealing with stress, confusion, pain, or pressure that you'll never see.

When you start to see the world this way, you become **calmer**, **kinder**, and more in control.

You stop wasting your energy on rage.
And you save it for your **real goals**—your growth, your peace, your purpose.

Daily Action:

> ➤ When something upsets you today, pause and ask: **"Is this just an empty boat?"**
> ➤ Respond with patience, not impulse.
> ➤ Remind yourself: **"Most people are not against me—they're just drifting."**

CAPSULE 14

Three Questions That Change Everything

"Clarity begins where your pen ends."

Sometimes, you don't need advice.
You just need the **right question.**

Not from a book.
Not from a teacher.
But from yourself—written with honesty.

Here are **three journaling prompts** that can shake your thinking, open your heart, and help you see your true path more clearly.

Question 1: What would you attempt if you knew you couldn't fail?

Let your imagination run.
No fear. No limits.
What dream is hiding behind your fear of failing?

Would you start a business?
Write a book?
Pursue your dream career?
Stand on a stage and teach?

This question tells you what your heart truly wants.

Question 2: What would you do if you knew you would fail… but you'd still do it anyway?

This one goes deeper.

Because some things are worth doing—even without a guarantee.
Even if no one watches.
Even if you never win.

This reveals your **passion**.
What do you care about so much that you'd do it regardless of the outcome?

Question 3: If the way you lived this week became the way you lived every week... would you be proud of that life?

This one stings. In a good way.

Did you use your time wisely?
Did you live with energy?
Did you study with focus?
Did you make time for things that matter?

This one tells you if you're **living in alignment**—or drifting.

Lessons in the Quiet

These three questions aren't just about motivation.
They're about **truth**.
About finding what really matters to you—and gently
realigning yourself with it.

Journaling is not a waste of time.
It's a meeting with your future self.

You don't need perfect answers.
You just need to be honest.

Take 15 minutes this week.
Write your answers without judgment.

You might just discover...
What's holding you back
What's worth chasing
And what's already beautiful about your life

Daily Action:

> ➢ Choose one question and write your honest
> response today.
> ➢ Ask yourself: "Am I living toward my answers, or
> away from them?"
> ➢ Revisit these every few weeks—you'll be amazed
> how your answers evolve.

CAPSULE 15

The Pygmalion Effect

"People rise to the expectations placed upon them."

This is Robert Rosenthal. In 1968, alongside a school principal named **Lenore Jacobson**, he made a discovery that could change your life.

They conducted a study in a school where teachers were told that certain students—based on an "IQ test"—were expected to bloom academically over the next year.

But here's the twist: those students were picked **completely at random**.

There was no special test. No real reason behind their names being selected. Just chance.

Yet by the end of the academic year, those randomly selected students had actually **performed better**.

Not because they suddenly became more intelligent. Not because they were secretly brilliant.

But because their **teachers believed** they would do well.

That belief changed the way the teachers treated them:

- ➢ More attention
- ➢ More encouragement
- ➢ More feedback
- ➢ More patience

And over time, the students began to live up to those expectations.

This phenomenon is called the **Pygmalion Effect**—named after the mythological sculptor who carved a statue so beautiful that he fell in love with it, and it eventually came to life.

The idea is simple:

- ➤ **We perform better when others expect us to.**
- ➤ **We perform worse when others expect us to fail.**

And this applies everywhere:
Not just in schools, but in **workplaces, friendships, families**, and most importantly—in your relationship with **yourself.**

Lessons in the Quiet

Let's get honest: How often have you lowered your standards... because you thought you weren't capable of more? How many times have you underperformed... simply because no one ever expected you to shine?

The truth is, **what we expect—shapes what we become**.

If you see yourself as average, you'll perform like you are. If people around you speak to you like you can't succeed, a part of you might start believing it.

That's how quiet, invisible expectations shape your reality.

But here's the best part of the Pygmalion Effect: It works in reverse, too.

Step 1: Change your inner voice

Start expecting more from yourself. Not in a cruel, unrealistic way—but in a **believing**, encouraging way.

Say to yourself:

> "I'm capable of scoring over 90 marks."
> "I'm becoming more disciplined every day."
> "I can understand this concept, even if it's tough right now."

Your brain listens. Your actions follow.

Step 2: Upgrade your circle

Surround yourself with people who:

- Cheer for your efforts
- Expect consistency from you
- Don't let you quit too easily

Because when you're around low-expectation environments, you shrink to fit them. But when you're around **growth-minded people**, you stretch to meet them.

Look around: Who expects you to win? And deeper still: Do **you** expect yourself to?

Because expectations—spoken or silent—become the script your life follows. And you, my friend, get to be the author.

Daily Action:

- ➢ Write down 3 areas where you've been setting the bar too low.
- ➢ Rewrite those expectations in a voice that believes in you.
- ➢ Reflect on your circle: Who pushes you to grow? Who holds you back?

Remind yourself daily: *"I rise to the level of belief I place in myself—and surround myself with."*

CAPSULE 16

The Chinese Farmer

"Maybe. Maybe not. Let life unfold."

Once upon a time, there was a Chinese farmer.

One day, his **horse ran away**.
The villagers rushed to his house and said,
"Oh no, what terrible luck!"
The farmer replied,
"Maybe."

The next day, the horse returned—bringing **seven wild horses** with it.
The villagers said,
"Amazing! What good fortune!"
The farmer replied,
"Maybe."

On the third day, the farmer's son tried to ride one of the new horses.
He fell and **broke his leg**.
Again, the villagers said,
"Oh no, how unlucky!"
The farmer simply said,
"Maybe."

On the fourth day, the army came to recruit young men for war.
Because the son had a broken leg, they left him behind.
The villagers said,
"How fortunate you are!"

The farmer—again—replied:
"Maybe."

That's it.
That's the whole story.

But inside this simple tale is one of the deepest life lessons of all.

Lessons in the Quiet

We all go through **ups and downs**.

You miss a deadline.
You fail a test.
You get stuck in traffic, or lose an opportunity, or hear something you didn't want to hear.

And your mind instantly shouts:
"This is bad. This is unfair. Why me?"

But truthfully?
You don't know what it means yet.

Sometimes the thing that feels like a failure today turns out to be **a turning point tomorrow**.
And sometimes what feels like a win today comes with lessons you weren't ready for.

That's the **wisdom of the Chinese farmer**:

Life is complex.
Outcomes are unpredictable.
And labeling every event as *"good"* or *"bad"* too quickly...
often leads us to unnecessary stress, overreaction, and wasted energy.

Instead of clinging to what *should have happened*, try saying:

> **"Maybe."**
> **"Let's see what comes next."**
> **"I'll grow through this."**

This mindset doesn't make life easy.
But it does make it **lighter**.

And it allows you to focus on what you **can control**—your attitude, your actions, and your next step.

Daily Action:

> ➤ Think of one recent event that frustrated or disappointed you.
> ➤ Say: *"Maybe. Let's see what comes next."*
> ➤ Write down what you can learn from it—or how it might turn out to be part of something bigger.

CAPSULE 17

The Region-Beta Paradox

"Sometimes good enough is what holds you back."

Meet Jim.

Jim commutes to work.
If the office is **less than a mile away**, he **walks**.
If it's **more than a mile**, he **cycles**.

Seems simple, right?

But here's where it gets weird:
When Jim's office is **two miles** away, he cycles—and gets there **faster** than if it were closer.

Why?

Because **being slightly worse off** pushed him to take **more effective action**.

This is the **Region-Beta Paradox**, discovered by psychologist **Daniel Gilbert**.

"Region Beta" is a strange zone where worse situations actually lead to **better outcomes**—because they trigger action.

And it's not just about distance or commuting.

It shows up everywhere in life.

Lessons in the Quiet

Let's say your job is just okay.
Not exciting, but not miserable.
So you stay.
For years.

But what if it was awful?
So bad you couldn't ignore it?

Then you'd be forced to take action—
To quit. Change. Rebuild.
And maybe… finally chase the thing you actually want.

That's Region-Beta.

When something is *barely tolerable*, it becomes
comfortable enough to trap you.
You don't complain. But you also don't grow.
You tell yourself: "It's fine." And you stop aiming for better.

This shows up in:

> ➢ Relationships that don't excite but don't hurt
> ➢ Jobs that pay just enough but drain your soul
> ➢ Study routines that keep you busy but never move the needle
> ➢ Health habits that aren't terrible—but aren't good either

You wait for things to get worse—before you give yourself permission to act.

But what if you didn't wait?

What if you left "barely okay" behind—and chose better
before things collapsed?

Daily Action:

> - Ask yourself: "Where in my life am I *stuck in 'just fine'?"*
> - If this area suddenly got *worse*, what action would I take?
> - Why not take it now?

CAPSULE 18

The Broken Window Theory

"Small problems ignored become big problems later."

In the 1980s, crime rates in New York City were high. Streets were unsafe, subways were covered in graffiti, and many buildings stood in disrepair. But something unexpected began to shift when a few researchers and city officials noticed a strange pattern.

They called it the **Broken Window Theory.**

They observed that when a single window on a building was broken and **left unrepaired**, something predictable happened:

- People walked by and assumed the building was abandoned.
- Vandals added graffiti.
- Trash piled up around the sidewalk.
- Eventually, more windows were broken.
- And within weeks, the entire block started to decay.

But here's what was truly fascinating: When that **first window** was repaired **immediately**, the opposite occurred:

- People respected the building.
- Crime in that area dropped.
- The surroundings stayed cleaner.

> ➢ And the environment felt safe, even before any major reform.

What began as a **small act of maintenance** had a ripple effect. It wasn't about repairing windows—it was about **repairing signals**.

When something looks neglected, people assume **no one cares.** But when something is clean, organized, and cared for, it sends a different message: **"These matters."**

This one insight helped reshape how New York tackled crime—starting not with big policies, but with tiny details. Graffiti was removed from subways. Streets were cleaned. Broken windows were repaired quickly. And slowly, order returned.

What began as a **small act of maintenance** had a ripple effect. It wasn't about repairing windows—it was about **repairing signals**.

Lessons in the Quiet

This theory doesn't just apply to cities.
It applies to **you**.

- ➤ That messy desk you stopped cleaning.
- ➤ That one workout you skipped (which turned into three).
- ➤ That tiny pile of books you'll "sort later."
- ➤ That email you avoided replying to.

At first, it feels harmless.
But slowly, those little cracks spread.
They send a message to your subconscious:

> "Standards don't matter."
> "Order isn't important."
> "I can let this slide."

And soon, your **environment**, your **mindset**, and your **momentum** start to fall apart.

This isn't about being a perfectionist.
It's about being a **protector of your standards**.

High achievers often seem obsessed with the small things.
Why? Because they know that small messes lead to bigger ones.
And small wins lead to massive change.

So here's the question:

What's your broken window right now?

And what would change if you fixed it **today**?

Daily Action:

> ➢ Look around your environment—home, desk, inbox, routine.
> ➢ Identify **one "broken window"** you've been ignoring.
> ➢ Fix it. Clean it. Respond to it. Reset it.
> ➢ Let your action say: **"This space matters. I matter."**

CAPSULE 19

Right Talent, Wrong Audience

"You're not always overlooked. Sometimes, you're just in the wrong place."

Meet **Joshua Bell**—one of the most celebrated violinists in the world.

A child prodigy from the age of four, Joshua trained relentlessly for years.
He performed at the most prestigious concert halls.
He sold out theaters.
He played with a **$3.5 million violin**—an antique masterpiece crafted by Stradivarius.

Two days before this story takes place, he had filled an entire theater in Boston.
Standing ovation. Thunderous applause.

But then...
Joshua Bell tried something radical.

He dressed in plain clothes.
Put on a baseball cap.
And stood at the entrance of a busy **Washington, D.C. subway station.**

He opened his violin case.
And began to play.

Not just any tune—he performed one of the **most difficult, intricate pieces ever written.**

For 45 minutes, the music echoed through the subway.

Master-level technique.
Passion.
Precision.
A violin worth millions.

And yet?

Over **1,000 people** walked by.
Only **7** stopped.
He earned **$32.17** in total tips.

Lessons in the Quiet

What changed?

Not his talent.
Not the music.
Not the instrument.

Just the **setting**.
Just the **audience**.

This story isn't just about Joshua Bell.
It's about all of us.

At some point, you'll feel invisible.
You'll pour your heart into your work—and no one will clap.
You'll submit your best work—and it'll be ignored.
You'll show up with full passion—and feel like it didn't matter.

But here's the truth:

It's not always your fault.
It's not that you're not good enough.
Sometimes, **you're just in the wrong room.**

The world doesn't always reward you immediately.
And sometimes, the people around you aren't equipped to **recognize your brilliance**.

But that doesn't mean you stop playing.
That doesn't mean your gift isn't valuable.

Because the same music that was ignored in the subway...
was celebrated in the concert hall.

So keep creating.
Keep growing.
Keep showing up.

Your audience might not be here **yet**.
But they're out there.

Daily Action:

> ➤ Reflect: Have you ever felt overlooked despite giving your best?
> ➤ Ask: Am I in the right room? Or just the wrong one?
> ➤ Commit: No matter who's watching—**keep mastering your craft**.

CAPSULE 20

The Arrival Fallacy

"You don't arrive at happiness. You practice it."

You tell yourself:

"I'll be happy once I clear the exam."
"I'll feel confident once I get that job."
"I'll finally rest when I hit my goal."
"I'll enjoy life after I succeed."

This is what psychologists call **The Arrival Fallacy**.

It's the belief that once you arrive at a certain destination—success, status, recognition—you'll finally feel **complete**.
Finally satisfied.
Finally at peace.

But here's what actually happens:

> You hit the goal.
> You get the result.
> You feel happy—for a moment.

And then?

A new target appears.
A new insecurity shows up.
A new voice in your head whispers:
"Now what?"

Because it turns out:
Achievement doesn't equal fulfillment.

Success doesn't fix your self-worth.
Arrival doesn't end the journey.

Lessons in the Quiet

The human brain is wired for growth, not arrival.
Once we get what we want, we naturally want more.

And if you're not careful, you'll spend your whole life
postponing joy—waiting for a finish line that keeps
moving.

But what if joy wasn't waiting **after** the goal?

What if it was found **in the process**?

> ➤ In solving just one mock test today.
> ➤ In understanding one concept clearly.
> ➤ In showing up consistently, even when motivation
> is low.
> ➤ In learning to **like yourself during the climb**, not
> just at the summit.

That's not giving up on success.
That's making sure **you're not empty when you get
there**.

Because if you can't enjoy the journey, you'll never enjoy
the destination.
And if you hate who you are on the way up, you won't
magically love yourself at the top.

Daily Action:

> ➤ Ask yourself: "What am I waiting for to feel
> happy?"
> ➤ Practice presence: Find *one thing today* to enjoy,
> without needing to achieve anything.
> ➤ Remind yourself: **Success is a moment.
> Fulfillment is a mindset.**

CAPSULE 21

Commitment Device Theory

"Make it easier to win—and harder to escape."

You want to do it.
You *mean* to do it.
You even write it in your planner:

"I'll wake up at 5 AM."
"I'll revise this topic tonight."
"I'll finish that mock test by Sunday."

But when the moment comes...
You scroll.
You snooze.
You postpone.

Why does that happen?

Because your **future self is unreliable.**

When you make plans, you're motivated. Energized.
But the *future version* of you is tired. Distracted. Tempted.

So how do you beat this?

Enter: the **Commitment Device**.

It's a behavioral trick that makes your *future self* stick to
your *current goals*.
You create friction around quitting—and make it easier to
follow through.

Here's how it works:

Want to study in the morning? Sleep with your book and highlighters next to your bed.
Want to stop phone use at night? Give it to a family member after 9 PM.
Want to stay consistent with mock tests? Announce your test schedule publicly to your group.

Now, even if your future self *wants* to quit—it's not so easy. You've locked the escape door behind you.

Lessons in the Quiet

We often think success is about willpower.
But real progress comes from **designing your environment** so that good choices are automatic.

Top athletes do it.
Writers do it.
Even tech companies use commitment devices on *you*—notifications, streaks, check-ins.
Why not use it **for yourself**?

The smartest students don't always have more discipline.
They have **better systems**.

So the next time you set a goal, don't just write it down.

> ➤ Build a wall around it.
> ➤ Add a cost to quitting.
> ➤ Make the right choice the easiest one.

Because when your motivation dips—and it will—your environment will catch you.

And that's how ordinary people build extraordinary habits.

Daily Action:

> ➤ Choose one goal you're serious about.
> ➤ Create a simple *commitment device* today: a public promise, a locked distraction, a set routine.
> ➤ Let it protect you from your future self.

CAPSULE 22

Healed by the Mind

"Your imagination can be medicine."

There was a father.

His son had fallen gravely ill.
The doctors had tried everything.
The condition was rare. Incurable. Hopeless, they said.

But this father believed in something deeper than medicine.
He believed in the **subconscious mind**—and its incredible power to heal.

So he made a decision.
Every night, before falling asleep, he would close his eyes...
and **visualize his son completely healed**.

He didn't beg.
He didn't worry.
He didn't plead with desperation.

He saw the outcome in his mind **as if it had already happened**.

He imagined his son running, laughing, playing in full health.
He felt the joy, the gratitude, the peace of seeing him well again.

He did this **consistently**, with faith and emotion.
He fed the image to his subconscious until it became **reality within**.

And then, something incredible happened:

His son got better.
Bit by bit. Day by day.
Until he was fully healed—against every medical prediction.

Was it magic? No.
It was the **law of belief and repetition**—working through the subconscious mind.

Lessons in the Quiet

Your subconscious doesn't know the difference between what is **real** and what is **vividly imagined**.

When you imagine something with feeling and repetition, it begins to believe it's true.
And when belief becomes strong enough, it begins to shape **your reality**.

This doesn't just apply to healing.

> ➤ Visualize yourself **understanding complex topics**.
> ➤ Visualize yourself **marking correct answers with confidence**.
> ➤ Visualize yourself **receiving that congratulatory message** after clearing UGC NET.

Don't just hope.
See it. Feel it. Believe it.

Your mind becomes a mirror—and your life reflects what you impress upon it.

This is not delusion.
This is *deliberate creation*.

If you feed your mind fear, it will grow panic.
If you feed it faith, it will grow power.

So feed it well.

Daily Action:

> ➤ Tonight, before bed, close your eyes and visualize one goal as **already accomplished**.
> ➤ Feel the joy, peace, and excitement of that success.

> ➢ Repeat it daily. Speak it into your subconscious.

Your imagination is not fiction. It's rehearsal.

85

CAPSULE 23

The Voice Within

"If you speak fear to your mind, it listens. But if you speak confidence, it follows."

He was a talented actor.

Smart. Trained. Passionate.

But every time he stepped on stage, his body betrayed him.

His heart would pound.
His throat would tighten.
His memory would go blank.

It was called **stage fright**, and it was ruining everything he had worked for.

He tried tips. Techniques. Breathing exercises.

Nothing lasted.

Until one day, he discovered the power of the **subconscious mind**—and how words repeated with emotion can **reshape your identity**.

He created a simple affirmation:
"I radiate confidence and poise. I am calm. I am in control."

Every day, multiple times a day, he repeated it.
In the mirror. In the car. Before rehearsals. Before bed.

At first, it felt fake. But he kept going.

And day by day, something began to shift.
The fear softened. The panic faded.
And confidence quietly returned.

He wasn't pretending anymore.
He had **reprogrammed** the belief system deep inside.

When he stepped on stage weeks later, he delivered a flawless performance.

Not because the fear had vanished—but because he had built a stronger inner voice.

Lessons in the Quiet

You don't need to be an actor to feel stage fright.

Every student, teacher, professional, or speaker has faced it.

That test that freezes your mind.
That crowd that makes your palms sweat.
That doubt that whispers: "You're not good enough."

But here's the truth:

Your mind listens to what you **repeatedly say to it**.

If you tell it "I can't do this," it obeys.
If you tell it "I am prepared. I am capable," it rewires.

Affirmations aren't magic spells.
They're **mental training**—like lifting weights for your self-image.

Say them enough times, with enough conviction… and they become true.

So, choose your script wisely.

Daily Action:

> ➤ Write down 1 affirmation that speaks to the fear you want to overcome.
> ➤ Say it **3 times a day**, with energy and belief.
> ➤ When fear shows up, speak louder.

The most important words you'll ever hear… are the ones you say to yourself.

CAPSULE 24

The Rejected Bestseller

"Rejection isn't the end—it's the test."

Long before the wizarding world captivated millions, **Joanne Rowling** sat in a small apartment with a baby in one arm and a manuscript in the other.

She was broke.
Unemployed.
Battling depression.
Living on government support.
And writing in cafés when she could afford the coffee.

Her manuscript?
A magical story about a boy with a lightning scar and a hidden destiny.

She believed in it with all her heart.
So she sent it to publishers.

One rejection came.
Then another.
And another.
Twelve publishers said no.

They said the story was too long.
Too strange.
Not commercial enough.
One even tossed it in the trash without reading it.

But she didn't stop.
Because deep down, she knew: **the story mattered.**

Finally, a small publishing house, Bloomsbury, said yes—**only after the editor's 8-year-old daughter read the manuscript and begged for more.**

Today, **J.K. Rowling's Harry Potter series has sold over 500 million copies**, been translated into over 80 languages, and inspired an entire generation of readers and dreamers.

Lessons in the Quiet

Every rejection feels personal.
Every "no" stings.

But sometimes rejection is not a signal to stop—it's a **filter** to test your persistence.

If Rowling had stopped at the first rejection, we'd never know Hogwarts.
If you stop after one failed attempt, the world may never see **your magic**.

People may not understand your vision at first.
The system may overlook you.
The road may be longer than you expected.

But if the **dream feels real**, don't let anyone's "no" become your full stop.

Rejection doesn't mean you're wrong.
It means you haven't found the right door yet.

Daily Action:

> ➢ Think of one dream or idea you've put aside after rejection.
> ➢ Revisit it today—with fresh eyes and firmer belief.
> ➢ Tell yourself: **"It only takes one yes."**

Believe in your Hogwarts—even if others don't see the magic yet.

CAPSULE 25

The Man Who Lit Up the World

"Every wrong attempt discarded is another step forward." — Thomas Edison

Have you ever been called "slow," "average," or "hopeless"?
Have you failed a test? Lost a job? Forgotten the answer to a simple question in front of everyone?

Then you have something in common with **Thomas Edison**.

Yes—the man who gave us the electric light bulb.
The man who holds **over 1,000 patents**.
The man whose inventions shaped the modern world.

But his early life?
It was anything but successful.

His teachers said he was **"too dumb to learn anything."**
He struggled in school.
He dropped out by the age of **12**.
He got fired from multiple jobs—once for spilling acid on his boss's desk!

And don't even get started on the light bulb.
He didn't create it in one go.

He **failed over 1,000 times.**

Most people would've stopped at failure number 5.
Or 50.
Or 500.

But Edison didn't see failure the way most people do.

He said:

"I have not failed. I've just found 10,000 ways that won't work."

To him, failure wasn't the end.
It was **information.**
It was **progress.**
It was a **step closer to the answer.**

Lessons in the Quiet

We often treat failure like a final verdict.
One mistake and we start believing we're not good enough.
One rejection, and we shrink our dreams.

But Edison shows us something powerful:

Failure doesn't define you.
It refines you.
It's not the opposite of success. It's a part of it.

That mock test you didn't pass?
That concept you keep getting wrong?
That one subject that makes you feel stuck?

It's not proof that you're weak.
It's proof that you're **learning**.

Imagine if Edison had stopped after 10 tries.
We'd still be using candles.
And we'd never know what was possible when **someone refuses to quit.**

So next time you feel discouraged, remember this:
Your failure is not a sign to stop.
It's a signal to keep going.

Daily Action:

> ➤ Write down your latest failure—or fear of failing.
> ➤ Next to it, write one thing you learned from it.
> ➤ Repeat: **"Every failure is just a step forward."**

Keep showing up. You're only one bright idea away from your breakthrough.

CAPSULE 26

The Old Man and the Sea

"A man can be destroyed—but not defeated." —
Ernest Hemingway

Meet Santiago.

An old Cuban fisherman.
Alone.
Exhausted.
And on the worst losing streak of his life.

For **84 days**, he sailed out to sea—and came back with
nothing.
No fish.
No luck.
Only whispers from the villagers…
"He's finished."
"His time has passed."
"Poor old man."

But Santiago didn't quit.

On the **85th day**, he set sail again.
Farther than he ever had before.
Into the open, dangerous waters.

And there, in the silence, he hooked the **biggest fish he
had ever seen**.

A marlin so massive, it dragged his boat for **three days**.
He was starving.
His hands were bleeding.
His body shaking.

But he held the line.
Alone.
Focused.
Unbroken.

When he finally killed the marlin, it was too big to bring
into his boat.
He tied it to the side.
But on the way back, **sharks attacked**.

They tore it apart—piece by piece—until nothing was left
but the skeleton.

He returned to shore with no prize.
Nothing to sell.
No proof of his struggle.

And yet?

He had fought.
He had endured.
And in that quiet, unwavering courage—he had **won**.

Lessons in the Quiet

You won't always be rewarded for your effort.
You won't always be seen.
You might study all night and still score less than you hoped.
You might give everything and come back empty-handed.

But like Santiago, you must keep sailing.
Keep showing up.
Keep fighting for the **dignity of the effort**.

Because success isn't always about trophies.
Sometimes it's about the quiet power of a person who refuses to quit—
Even when there's no audience.
Even when there's no applause.

Remember:
You are not your scoreboard.
You are your spirit.
You are your endurance.

The world may never fully know how hard you tried.
But *you* will.
And that's enough.

Daily Action:

- ➤ Reflect on a goal you're pursuing that's hard—but meaningful.
- ➤ Write down: "Even if I lose the marlin, I'll still return with strength."
- ➤ Remind yourself: **Your effort is the proof—not the prize.**

CAPSULE 27

Paradox of Choice

"More choices don't bring more freedom. They bring more doubt."

The Paradox of Choice

"When everything is possible, nothing feels certain." — Barry Schwartz

You walk into a store.
There's a table of jams.
One day, it has **6 flavours**.
Another day, it has **24**.

Guess when people actually bought more jam?
Not with 24.
With 6.

Why?
Because too many options **don't free us**—they **freeze us**.
This is what Barry Schwartz called **The Paradox of Choice**.

More choices seem like a gift.
But they often become a burden.
We hesitate.
We overthink.
We fear picking wrong.

This isn't just about jam.
It's about **choosing what to study**.
Picking a Netflix show.
Deciding on a job. A city. A life partner.

And the cruel twist?
Even after we choose, we're often less satisfied.
Because in the back of our mind is a whisper—
"Maybe the other one was better..."

But there's a way through.
It starts with **intentional simplicity**.
With understanding that the power isn't in having more.
It's in having **clarity**.

Lessons in the Quiet

You don't need every option.
You need the right one—for you.
Don't wait for the "perfect" choice.
It doesn't exist.
And chasing it will only lead to exhaustion.

Sometimes, **good enough is great**.
Sometimes, the key isn't choosing right—
But choosing **once**, and then going **all in**.

Remember:
Freedom isn't about endless options.
It's about the courage to commit.

Daily Action:

> ➤ Identify one area in your life where you're stuck in indecision.
> ➤ Cut down your options to **3 or fewer**.
> ➤ Choose one.
> ➤ Write: *"I choose this path—not because it's perfect, but because I'm ready."*

Clarity isn't a gift.
It's a decision.
Make it.

CAPSULE 28

Reticular Activating System—or RAS.

"Your brain listens to your goals—if you give it something to hear."

At the base of your brainstem, there's a small, often-ignored bundle of nerves that acts like your brain's personal gatekeeper.
It's called the **Reticular Activating System—or RAS**.

Tiny? Yes.
But powerful? Incredibly.

Every second, your brain is bombarded by **millions of sensory inputs**—sounds, colors, smells, faces, details.
Without a filter, you'd be overwhelmed.
That's where the RAS comes in.
It decides what's **important**—and what can be **ignored**.

And here's where it gets fascinating:
Your **RAS listens to your focus**.

Tell it what matters—and it will amplify that.
Ignore your goals—and it will filter them out.

Ever decided you wanted a Fiat 500?
Suddenly, you start seeing them **everywhere**—on roads, billboards, Instagram.
They were always there.
But now, your brain thinks they're relevant—because you told it so.

Here's another example:
You're scrolling through your phone.

You see a quote about starting a business.
Normally, you'd scroll past.
But today, you've been thinking about launching your own thing.
Suddenly, that quote feels personal.
It sticks.
That's your RAS at work—**tuning in to your focus**.

It's like Google for your brain.
You input the keyword…
And it starts searching your environment for matching results.

Lessons in the Quiet

Here's the life-changing part:
You can train your RAS—**on purpose**.

If you review your goals daily...
If you think about them, write them down, say them out loud...
You're **reprogramming your brain** to find alignment.

"Help me become healthier."
"Help me spot that business idea."
"Help me find people who uplift me."

And your brain, your RAS, begins to respond.

It starts filtering in **opportunities**, **ideas**, **connections**, and **resources** aligned with your goal.
Not by magic.
By **attention**.

But here's the trap:
Most people write down a goal once—and forget it.
Their RAS stops tuning in.
And so, life feels random. Unfocused. Uninspired.

You don't rise to the level of your potential.
You rise to the level of your programming.

And programming begins with **focus**.

Daily Action:

> ➤ **Write down your top 3 goals**. Keep them where you can see them—on your wall, mirror, phone lock screen.

➢ **Spend 30 seconds every day reading them aloud**—in the morning, before bed, or whenever you need direction.
➢ **Whisper to your brain**:

> *"This is who I want to become."*
> *"This is where I'm going."*
> *"This is what matters."*

Train your RAS.
Sharpen your filter.
Give your brain something clear to chase.

Because what you focus on... **grows**.

CAPSULE 29

Goal-Gradient Hypothesis

"Progress isn't just about momentum. It's about proximity."

In 1932, psychologist **Clark Hull** was observing rats in a maze.
He noticed something curious:
The rats ran **faster** the closer they got to the reward.
Sluggish in the beginning…
But sprinting at the end.

He called it the **Goal-Gradient Hypothesis**.
And it doesn't just apply to lab rats.

It applies to **you**.

Have you ever noticed how energized you feel in the final minutes of a workout?
How you suddenly pick up the pace during the last week of a project?
Or how motivated you feel when you see 90% of your course complete?

That's not coincidence.
That's psychology.
Your brain sees the finish line—and sends a jolt of energy.
A rush of "You're almost there. Don't stop now."

But here's the key insight:
You don't need to wait for the final stretch to feel that motivation.

You can create it—**by breaking your big goals into visible checkpoints**.

When your brain sees that a goal is **close**, it works harder to help you reach it.
But if the goal feels too far, your energy fades.
You lose steam.
You procrastinate.
Not because you're lazy—
But because the **reward feels distant**.

Lessons in the Quiet

Want to tap into the goal-gradient effect every day?

Stop measuring progress only in big leaps.
Start celebrating **small wins**.

Instead of "Write a book," aim for "Write 200 words."
Instead of "Get fit," aim for "Finish 10 push-ups."
Instead of "Clear all my debt," aim for "Pay off one small bill."

Each step you finish creates a sense of momentum.
Each checkpoint activates your internal engine.
And slowly, the finish line starts pulling you in.

You don't have to be fast from the start.
You just have to keep creating **visible progress**.

Because in motivation, **distance matters**.
And the closer you feel to the goal, the faster you'll move.

Daily Action:

- ➢ Take one big goal and **break it into 5 smaller milestones**.
- ➢ Track your progress visually—use a tracker, journal, app, or sticky notes.
- ➢ After each milestone, **pause and acknowledge**: *"I'm closer now. I'm moving."*

Motivation doesn't come from waiting.
It comes from seeing the gap shrink.
Make it visible.
Make it real.

And let your progress pull you forward.

CAPSULE 30

It's Never Too Late

"Some people retire at 65. Others restart."

At age 65, most people are winding down.
Thinking of pensions, rest, and rocking chairs.

But **Harland Sanders** had other plans.
He had a fried chicken recipe…
A white suit…
And a dream that refused to retire.

With nothing but a $105 social security check in hand, he hit the road.
His idea?
Offer his recipe to restaurants—and earn a small commission on every sale.

It was simple.
It was brilliant.
But no one cared.

He was rejected **1,009 times**.
That's not a typo.
One thousand and nine.

He slept in his car.
He knocked on door after door.
He kept his suit pressed, his pitch ready, and his hope alive.

And finally, someone said **yes**.

That "yes" became **Kentucky Fried Chicken**—
One of the biggest fast-food empires in the world.

But it didn't begin with applause.
It began with grit.
And it proved one thing:
It's never too late to start.
Only too late to stop trying.

Lessons in the Quiet

You are **not too old**.
You are **not too late**.
You are **not out of chances**.

You might be at an age where people expect you to "settle."
To be safe.
To stop dreaming.

But **your timeline is your own**.
And purpose doesn't check birth certificates.

Whether you're 25 or 65—
What matters is **what you're willing to begin**.

You're not here to prove your worth to everyone.
You're here to prove your commitment to yourself.

Rejections don't disqualify you.
Delays don't define you.
The only real failure is **giving up before the breakthrough**.

Daily Action:

- ➤ Write this down:
  "It's not too late. I still have time. I still have a dream."
- ➤ Think of one idea, passion, or project you've been putting off because of age or timing.
- ➤ Take **one small action today**—a call, a sketch, a plan, a post.

Because the clock doesn't decide when you're done.
You do.

CAPSULE 31

Hawthorne Effect

"Sometimes, the spotlight is all the motivation we need."

Have you ever noticed yourself working harder when your teacher walks by?
Or typing faster when your manager is near your desk?
Or even fixing your posture when someone glances your way?

That's not just coincidence.
It's called the **Hawthorne Effect**.

Back in the 1920s, researchers at the **Hawthorne Works** factory in Chicago wanted to study how lighting affected worker productivity.

So they changed the brightness.
Made it dim.
Made it bright.
Tried different shifts.

But no matter what they did—productivity **kept increasing**.

It wasn't the lights.
It was the **attention**.
The workers knew they were being observed.
And that awareness changed everything.

They felt noticed.
Important.
Accountable.

That tiny shift—**"I'm being watched"**—ignited effort, discipline, and pride.

Lessons in the Quiet

This isn't just about factories or formal studies.
It's about **human nature**.

We tend to **show up better** when we're being seen.
Not out of fear, but out of meaning.

When someone watches, we focus.
When someone cares, we commit.
When someone believes in us, we rise.

But here's the twist:
You don't always need a supervisor.
You can **be your own observer**.

Start showing up as if someone's watching.
The discipline.
The posture.
The intention.

And if it helps—
Share your goals.
Join accountability groups.
Track your progress publicly.
Let light in.
Because visibility creates **vitality**.

Daily Action:

> ➢ Choose one habit or goal where your motivation is fading.
> ➢ Add **accountability**:
>> → Tell a friend.
>> → Track it on your wall.
>> → Journal your effort daily.

> ➢ Whisper to yourself:
> *"Even when no one's watching—I am."*

Because awareness creates alignment.
And sometimes, all it takes to level up…
Is knowing **you're seen**.

CAPSULE 32

Expectancy Theory

"You don't lack motivation. You lack belief in the outcome."

Imagine two people given the same task.
Same deadline.
Same tools.
Same environment.

One gives it their all.
The other just coasts through.

Why?

According to psychologist **Victor Vroom**, it's not about laziness.
It's about **expectancy**—a powerful internal formula that decides how much effort you'll give.

Vroom's **Expectancy Theory** says your motivation is a three-part equation:

1. **Effort-to-Performance Expectancy** — *"Can I actually do this?"*
   If you don't believe in your ability, your energy fades.
   But if you think your effort can lead to success, you lean in harder.

2. **Instrumentality** — *"Will it matter if I do well?"*
   If you think no one will notice or reward your effort, you'll hold back.
   But if you believe your hard work will lead to

recognition, opportunity, or results—you push forward.

3. **Valence** — *"Do I even want the reward?"*
    If the outcome doesn't excite you, it won't move you.
    But if the reward feels **personal, meaningful, or life-changing**, it pulls you toward action.

The truth is:
You won't go the extra mile **unless the road feels real, rewarding, and reachable**.

Lessons in the Quiet

Next time you find yourself procrastinating or half-heartedly working—don't beat yourself up.
Instead, ask:

Do I believe I can do this?
Do I think it will lead to something valuable?
Do I care about the reward?

If the answer to any of these is "No," your motivation will stall.
But here's the good news—
You can shift all three:

Build confidence by starting small and celebrating early wins.
Create meaning by linking effort to personal goals.
Redefine rewards—make them exciting, even if they're self-given.

Because motivation isn't magic.
It's **math**.

Daily Action:

> ➢ Choose one task you've been avoiding.
> ➢ Write answers to these:
>   1. *Can I do this?* → (What skill/step do I need?)
>   2. *Will it matter?* → (What result can this lead to?)
>   3. *Is the reward worth it?* → (What's in it for me?)

If the answers are weak—**upgrade them.**
Find new meaning.
Find new fuel.

Because once the equation makes sense,
effort becomes automatic.

CAPSULE 33

Hertzberg's Two-Factor Theory

"If you want people to do a good job, give them a good job to do."

In the 1950s, psychologist **Frederick Herzberg** wanted to understand what truly motivates people at work.

So he asked 200 professionals—engineers and accountants—about the **best** and **worst** moments of their jobs.
And what he discovered flipped traditional management thinking on its head.

Herzberg found that there were **two different kinds of factors** at play:

1. Hygiene Factors – the basics.

These don't excite you, but if they're missing, you'll feel miserable.
Think:
Salary
Working conditions
Company policies
Job security

These are like **oxygen.**
You don't notice it when it's there,
But when it's missing, you can't breathe.

They prevent dissatisfaction—
But they **don't create passion**.

2. Motivator Factors – the spark.

These are what make people light up, take initiative, and give their best.
Think:
Achievement
Personal growth
Recognition
Advancement

They're the reason someone stays late not because they have to—but because they **want** to.

Herzberg's message was clear:
You can't buy loyalty with paychecks alone.
You have to offer **purpose**.

Lessons in the Quiet

Motivation isn't just about **removing pain**.
It's about **creating meaning**.

A comfortable office won't make someone care.
But a challenge that stretches them?
A heartfelt "well done"?
A chance to grow?

That's where real motivation lives.

Even in your own life—
Notice what truly drives you.

It's not just about being "treated well."
It's about being **trusted**, **challenged**, and **recognized**.

So if you're a leader—don't just offer perks.
Offer purpose.
And if you're an individual—don't just chase comfort.
Chase **meaningful effort**.

Daily Action:

> ➤ Reflect on your current work or goals.
> ➤ Ask yourself:
>   → *Do I have the basics covered? (hygiene)*
>   → *But more importantly, do I feel challenged and appreciated? (motivators)*
> ➤ Write down one way you can add more **meaning or growth** to your current task.
>   → Take initiative.
>   → Ask for feedback.
>   → Set a mini-challenge.

Because comfort creates calm.
*But **meaning creates movement**.*

CAPSULE 34

Maslow's Hierarchy of Need

"Before you become your best self—you must first feel safe, seen, and supported."

In 1943, psychologist **Abraham Maslow** gave us a simple but powerful map of human motivation.
A **pyramid** with five levels.
From the ground up, it explained how we grow—not just physically, but emotionally, socially, and spiritually.

At the base are your **survival needs**:

- Food
- Water
- Shelter

Next comes **safety**:

- Health
- Stability
- Protection

Then, **love and belonging**:

- Relationships
- Family
- Connection

Followed by **esteem**:

- Respect
- Confidence
- Recognition

And at the top?
Self-actualization—
Becoming everything you're capable of.
The fullest version of you.
Not just surviving.
Thriving.

But here's the key insight:
You **can't skip steps**.
You can't chase your dream if you're starving.
You can't feel confident if you feel alone.
You can't build your best life on an unstable foundation.

And yet—many workplaces, schools, and even people
forget this.

But not **Chip Conley**, founder of Joie de Vivre Hotels.
He used Maslow's pyramid to **transform employee
motivation**.

Instead of treating his staff like task-doers, he treated them
like human beings.
In one retreat, he asked housekeepers:
"If a Martian saw what you do, what would they call you?"

Their answers?
"The Serenity Sisters"
"The Clutter Busters"
"The Peace of Mind Police"

They weren't just cleaning rooms.
They were creating **safety**.
Peace.
Belonging for strangers far from home.

That's Maslow's pyramid—**in action**.

Lessons in the Quiet

Too often, we try to *achieve* before we've learned to *heal*.
We aim for success—without security.
We crave growth—without grounding.

But motivation starts with **meeting your needs**.

Are you taking care of your body?
Do you feel safe in your space and choices?
Are you surrounded by people who care?
Do you recognize your own worth?

Only then can you reach the top—
Where goals feel aligned, and life feels whole.

And if you're leading others—
Remember: before you ask for performance,
Ask if their pyramid is intact.

Daily Action:

> ➢ Reflect on where you are in the pyramid today.
> → *Am I struggling at the base?*
> → *Or ready to climb higher?*
> ➢ Choose one unmet need—physical, emotional, or social—and take one action today to support it.
> ➢ If you're leading a team, ask yourself:
> → *Am I helping them feel safe, seen, and valued?*

Because the best version of you doesn't come from pressure—
It comes from **fulfillment**.

CAPSULE 35

Three-Dimensional Theory of Attribution

"It's not just what happened—it's how you understand what happened."

Two people fail the same test.
One walks away discouraged.
The other walks away determined.

What made the difference?

Psychologist **Bernard Weiner** believed the answer lies in **attribution**—how we explain our successes and failures. He developed a model with **three dimensions** that influence motivation:

1. Stability — *Is this always going to be this way?*

Let's say you aced a presentation.

If you tell yourself,
"I did well because I'm experienced,"
that's a **stable** cause. Your confidence grows.

But if you think,
"I just got lucky this time,"
that's **unstable**. You begin to doubt future outcomes.

The result?
Stable beliefs reinforce momentum.
Unstable ones create hesitation.

2. Locus of Control — *Whose hands is this in?*

When you earn a promotion and say,
"I worked hard for this,"
you feel powerful. Motivated.

But if you say,
"It was just office politics,"
you give away your power. Motivation drops.

Your belief about **who's in control** determines whether you stay engaged—or check out.

3. Controllability — *Can I change it next time?*

If your startup fails and you think,
"Next time, I'll try a better strategy,"
you're in growth mode.

But if you think,
"The market just wasn't right, nothing I could do,"
you become passive.

Feeling in control fuels action.
Feeling helpless kills momentum.

Lessons in the Quiet

Life is full of wins and setbacks.
But the way you **frame them** decides whether you spiral
or rise.

When you hit a wall, pause and ask:

Was this a one-time thing or a pattern? *(Stability)*
Was it up to me, or out of my hands? *(Locus of control)*
Can I do something differently next time? *(Controllability)*

The more power you give to your **effort**, **strategy**, and
growth,
the more power you reclaim over your **future**.

Failures don't have to define you—
They can **refine** you.

Daily Action:

- ➤ Think of one recent success or failure.
- ➤ Journal your answers to these three:
  - → *Was the cause stable or unstable?*
  - → *Was it internal or external?*
  - → *Was it controllable or uncontrollable?*
- ➤ Then reframe it:
  - → *"I can learn from this. I have influence. I can adjust."*

Because success begins not with what you do—
But with **how you think** about what you did.

CAPSULE 36

Pavlov Classical Conditioning

"Not every reaction is a choice. Some are conditioned responses."

In the early 1900s, Russian physiologist **Ivan Pavlov** made a discovery that would reshape how we understand human behavior.

He wasn't studying psychology.
He was studying digestion—specifically, dogs' saliva.

But something strange happened.

Even before the dogs saw food, they started drooling.
Just hearing the footsteps of the lab assistant was enough.

So Pavlov ran an experiment.
He rang a bell every time he gave the dogs food.
At first, the bell meant nothing.
But after a few repetitions...
The dogs began salivating **just from the sound of the bell**—even if no food followed.

This became known as **Classical Conditioning**.

In simple terms:
🔔 Neutral stimulus (bell) + 🦴 Meaningful stimulus (food) = 🐶 Conditioned response (salivation)
Eventually, 🔔 alone = 🐶 Salivation

But here's the twist—
You are being conditioned all the time too.

Lessons in the Quiet

Ever felt anxious when your phone buzzes?
Energized by the gym playlist—before even working out?
Hungry when you see your favorite takeout logo?

That's classical conditioning in action.

⚡ Certain sounds, sights, places, or even people become
triggers—not by logic, but by **repetition**.
Your brain wires connections between a neutral cue and an
emotional or physical response.

The good news?
If you've been conditioned *into* fear, doubt, laziness...
You can condition yourself *out* of it too.

Rewire the response.
Reclaim the trigger.
You're not a slave to your patterns—unless you choose to
be.

Daily Action:

> ➤ Identify one **trigger** in your life that leads to a
> negative response.
>> → A tone of voice, a notification, a place, a habit.
> ➤ Replace it with a **new association**.
>> → Add calming music, a motivating affirmation, a
>> new environment.
> ➤ Repeat the new pairing until the old association
> fades.

Because your reactions aren't permanent.
They're **trained**.
And that means...
You can retrain them.

134

CAPSULE 37

Skinner Operant Conditioning

"We repeat what's rewarded. We avoid what's punished."

In the 1930s, psychologist **B.F. Skinner** built a box.
Inside it, a hungry rat.
On one wall—a lever.

When the rat accidentally pressed the lever, a food pellet dropped.
The rat was surprised at first.
Then it tried again.
And again.
Eventually, it learned:
Press lever = Get food.

Skinner called this **Operant Conditioning**—
The idea that behavior is shaped by **consequences**.

Unlike Pavlov's **classical conditioning**, where responses are automatic,
Operant conditioning is about choices.

And the formula is simple:

- **Positive reinforcement** → Add something good = Behavior increases
- **Negative reinforcement** → Remove something bad = Behavior increases
- **Positive punishment** → Add something bad = Behavior decreases

- **Negative punishment** → Remove something good
  = Behavior decreases

Skinner's rats pressed levers.
Humans do something similar.

We're constantly learning:
What earns praise
What brings pain
What gets attention
What leads to silence

And slowly, **our habits are formed**.

Lessons in the Quiet

Every time you skip your workout and nothing happens—
you've been **negatively reinforced**.
Every time you get praise for hard work—you've been
positively reinforced.
Every time your phone rewards you with likes, you're
being trained.
Every. Single. Day.

You're being conditioned.

But here's the key:
You can **become the trainer**.
You can reward the behavior you want to grow.
You can gently punish the behavior you want to let go.

You don't need more willpower.
You need better **systems of reinforcement**.

Daily Action:

- ➢ Choose one positive habit you want to build.
- ➢ Set up a **small reward** for completing it.
  → Watch a favorite video, check a box, share it with a friend.
- ➢ Choose one negative habit to reduce.
- ➢ Add a **gentle consequence** when it happens.
  → Delay gratification, track the slip, reduce distractions.

Remember:
Behavior doesn't change with pressure.
It changes with **patterns**.

Become your own behavior designer.
Because what you reward… **repeats**.

CAPSULE 38

Pyramid Parable

"Effort is noble. But without wisdom, it becomes wasted."

Long ago, a great Egyptian Pharaoh summoned his two young nephews—**Chuma** and **Azur**.

He gave them a challenge:
Each must build a Pyramid—alone.
Whoever completed it would earn early retirement, unlimited riches, and eternal honor.

Azur began right away.
He dragged stones with his bare hands, lifted them with raw strength, and pushed forward with sheer determination.
The progress was painfully slow.
But it was visible.

Chuma, on the other hand, seemed to vanish.
He wasn't building.
He wasn't sweating.
To Azur, it looked like **he had given up**.

But in the shadows, Chuma was designing something else—a **machine**.

Three years passed.
Azur had barely laid a few stones.
Then, Chuma returned—with a machine that **lifted and placed the stones with ease**.

In a week, he did what took Azur a year.
In two months, he built the second level.
And within **eight years**, at the age of **26**, Chuma completed his Pyramid.

The Pharaoh kept his word.
Chuma became a **king**.
A **scholar**.
A **legend**.

Azur?
He doubled down on brute strength.
He never stopped.
He never evolved.
And two levels before finishing—**he died of exhaustion**.

One brother toiled endlessly.
The other one **thought differently**.

Lessons in the Quiet

We've been taught to equate **hard work** with **honor**.
But effort without **strategy** is just glorified suffering.

How many Azurs are out there—
Grinding without growing?
Sprinting without direction?
Pushing stones that could've been lifted smarter?

Chuma didn't quit.
He simply paused to **build a better way**.

That's not laziness.
That's **leverage**.

In life, you can force every brick into place...
Or you can **step back**, observe, and **build your machine**.

You don't win by outworking everyone.
You win by **outthinking** them.

Daily Action:

> ➢ Ask yourself: *"Where am I still dragging stones?"*
> ➢ Take one task, goal, or habit and explore a
>   **smarter system** for it:
>   → Could tech help?
>   → Could delegation help?
>   → Could a new method make it easier?
> ➢ Write this down:
>   *"I don't just work hard—I work wise."*

Because the goal isn't just to **build your pyramid**...
It's to live long enough to **enjoy it**.

CAPSULE 39

Marshmallow Test

"Discipline is remembering what you want—later."

In the 1970s, psychologist **Walter Mischel** conducted a simple experiment with children at Stanford University. Each child was left alone in a room with a single marshmallow.

Then came the offer:
"If you can wait 15 minutes without eating it, I'll give you a **second marshmallow**."

Some kids stared.
Some sniffed.
Some gave in.
But others distracted themselves, sang songs, looked away—**and waited**.

Years later, researchers followed up.
And what they found was astonishing.

The kids who **waited** grew into adults who were more **successful, healthy**, and **emotionally stable**.
Why?
Because they had learned **self-control**—
The ability to **choose future reward over instant pleasure**.

This wasn't about marshmallows.
It was about **mastery over impulse**.

Lessons in the Quiet

You live in a world of instant everything—
Likes, texts, one-day deliveries, dopamine hits.

But true rewards?
They require **waiting, building,** and **sacrifice**.

You can eat the marshmallow now—
Or you can wait, and build a life that feeds your soul.

Think about it:
The body you want
The degree you dream of
The business you believe in
The relationship you crave

None of these come instantly.
They demand patience, persistence, and the ability to say:
"Not yet, but soon."

Waiting doesn't mean doing nothing.
It means doing the **right things**—without needing **instant validation**.

Daily Action:

- ➢ Identify one area of life where you're settling for a "first marshmallow."
- ➢ Replace it with a long-term reward:
  - → Skip the scroll = Read one page
  - → Delay the treat = Fuel your body
  - → Pause the impulse = Build your goal
- ➢ Write this:
  "I don't chase quick wins. I wait for what's worth it."

CAPSULE 40

Japanese philosophy of Ikigai

"When you live with purpose, energy becomes effortless."

In a small Japanese village called **Okinawa**, people live
unusually long, happy lives.
They're vibrant at 90.
Joyful at 100.
Some still working in gardens and teaching others at 110.

What's their secret?
It's not just diet or genetics.
It's something deeper.

They call it **Ikigai** —
Your *"reason for being."*

Not a job.
Not a goal.
But the thing that makes you feel... alive.

Imagine four circles overlapping:

1. **What you love**
2. **What you're good at**
3. **What the world needs**
4. **What you can be paid for**

In the center lies your Ikigai—
That sweet spot where passion, mission, profession, and
vocation **merge into one life purpose.**

Ikigai doesn't shout.
It whispers.
It's not urgent.
It's *essential*.

Lessons in the Quiet

Some people chase money—and burn out.
Some chase passion—and go broke.
Some serve others—and forget themselves.

But when you align all four, you stop chasing.
You start **flowing**.

Your work becomes meaning.
Your day becomes joy.
Your life becomes whole.

You don't need to find it overnight.
Ikigai is not a destination.
It's a **daily alignment**.

Start where you are.
Ask:

What lights me up?
What do people thank me for?
What problem am I wired to solve?

You might not quit your job tomorrow—
But you can **infuse purpose into what you already do.**

Even washing dishes can be sacred,
When it's part of something meaningful.

Daily Action:

- ➢ Draw four circles:
  - o What I love
  - o What I'm good at
  - o What the world needs
  - o What I can be paid for
- ➢ Find one area where two or more overlap.

> ➤ Take one small action to **move toward that center**.

Write this:
"I don't just live to exist. I live to align."

Because when you find your Ikigai—
You don't just live longer.
You live **truer**.

CAPSULE 41

Sisyphus Myth

*"The struggle itself toward the heights is enough
to fill a man's heart."*

In ancient Greek mythology, there was a man named
Sisyphus.
Clever. Defiant.
And punished by the gods for outsmarting death—twice.

His sentence?
To roll a giant boulder up a mountain...
Only to watch it roll back down—**for eternity**.

Day after day.
Year after year.
No finish line.
No applause.
Just endless repetition.

Most would call it **a curse**.

But centuries later, philosopher **Albert Camus** offered a
radical idea:

"One must imagine Sisyphus happy."

Why?
Because when you accept the absurdity of the task—
And still choose to show up,
You reclaim your power.

It's not about the rock.
It's about the **resolve**.

Lessons in the Quiet

Some days, your goals will feel like that boulder.
Pushing. Sliding. Starting over.

You might ask:
"What's the point?"
"Why try if it keeps slipping?"
"Why show up when progress disappears?"

But here's the answer:
Because **showing up is the point**.

Every rep at the gym
Every rough draft of your book
Every quiet day in business
Every silent act of healing

These aren't punishments.
They're proof of your perseverance.

You don't need a final reward to justify the work.
Sometimes, the effort **is** the victory.
And the courage to push again tomorrow…
is everything.

Daily Action:

- ➢ Name your "boulder" — the task that keeps slipping.
- ➢ Reframe it: *"This is not pointless. This is practice for my strength."*
- ➢ Push again today—not for perfection, but for **power in the process**.

Write this:
"Even if the rock rolls down, I will rise with it."

Because success is not always finishing the climb.
Sometimes, it's **never stopping the push.**

152

CAPSULE 42

Daedalus and Icarus

"Don't just dream of flying. Learn how to steer."

In the depths of a labyrinth, the brilliant inventor
Daedalus and his son **Icarus** were trapped.
There was no door.
No tunnel.
No key.

So Daedalus built **wings**—feathers held together with wax.
A way to **rise above the maze**.

Before takeoff, he gave his son one rule:
"Don't fly too high—the sun will melt the wax."
"Don't fly too low—the sea will soak the feathers."

Balance, he said.
That's how you escape.

But Icarus—young and thrilled by the taste of freedom—
soared too high.
The sun melted the wax.
The wings collapsed.
And Icarus fell—into the sea.

It's a tale often told as a warning against arrogance.
But there's more to it.

Because **ambition without awareness** is a recipe for ruin.

Lessons in the Quiet

In your own life, you may build wings—
Skills. Ideas. Dreams. Bold visions.

But wings alone aren't enough.

You need **discipline** to guide your ascent.
You need **humility** to watch the wind.
You need **self-awareness** to avoid burning out.

Icarus' mistake wasn't dreaming of the sky.
It was ignoring the balance between **limitless potential** and **real-world wisdom**.

Your journey isn't just about how high you fly.
It's about **how long you stay in the air**.

Don't let praise lift you too high.
Don't let fear pull you too low.
Learn to **navigate**.

Because success isn't found in the extremes—
It's found in the **centered flight**.

Daily Action:

- ➤ Identify one area where you're flying too high (overextending) or too low (playing small).
- ➤ Write this down:
  "Wings are power. Wisdom is control."
- ➤ Adjust your altitude:
  - → Rest if you're burning out.
  - → Stretch if you're underestimating yourself.

Balance is not playing it safe. It's **playing it smart**.

CAPSULE 43

The Long Way Home

"You can travel the world. But until you come back to yourself, you'll always feel lost."

After the fall of Troy, the warrior **Odysseus** set sail for home.
He had fought for ten years.
And now, all he wanted was to return to **Ithaca**—
To his wife **Penelope**, his son **Telemachus**, and the quiet peace of his kingdom.

But the gods had other plans.

A storm pulls him off course.
A Cyclops traps him in a cave.
Siren songs nearly lure him to his death.
A goddess offers him immortality.
A kingdom offers him comfort.

Yet through all of it—Odysseus keeps sailing.
Why?
Because **he never forgets where he belongs**.

It takes him ten more years to return.
He loses men.
He loses time.
He nearly loses himself.

But he holds onto one thing:
The **call to return**.

Not just to a place.
But to his **identity**, his **values**, and his **purpose**.

Lessons in the Quiet

In life, you'll be pulled in a thousand directions.
Success
Fame
Comfort
Distraction

Like Odysseus, you might drift.
You might fight monsters.
You might get stuck on islands that look like paradise—but feel like prisons.

But deep down, you'll hear the same call:

"Come home."

Home to your values.
Home to your purpose.
Home to the person you were before the world told you to be someone else.

Odysseus didn't just return to Ithaca.
He returned to **himself**.

And so can you.

Daily Action:

- ➤ Ask yourself: *What is my Ithaca?*
  → What goal, habit, or identity have I strayed from?
- ➤ Close your eyes and write this down:
  "I may wander, but I will not forget who I am."
- ➤ Take one small step today that brings you back to your **true path**.

Because life will offer you detours—
But only you can choose to return.

CAPSULE 44

The Ship and the Anchor

"You were built to sail, not to stay."

Imagine a ship—
Strong. Steady. Beautifully built.

It sits in the harbor,
tethered by a heavy anchor buried deep in the sand.

The waters beyond are open.
The winds are calling.
The stars are waiting to be chased.

But the ship does not move.

Not because it can't...
But because it won't let go.

The anchor is safe.
The harbor is familiar.
And the unknown—however vast—is uncertain.

The ship begins to rust.
Its sails, unused.
Its map, meaningless.

Because **even the most powerful vessel becomes powerless when tied to what it won't release**.

Lessons in the Quiet

You are the ship.

And somewhere in your life, there is an anchor.

A toxic habit
A relationship you've outgrown
A fear of failure
A belief that says, "I'm not ready."

You weren't born to stay docked in a harbor of hesitation.
You were made to move.
To discover.
To expand.

But first—you must know what's holding you down.

Anchors aren't always obvious.
Sometimes they look like love.
Sometimes they look like comfort.
Sometimes they look like "being responsible."

But if they keep you from growing,
they are not grounding you—they are **sinking you**.

You don't need to destroy the anchor.
You just need to **untie the rope**.

Daily Action:

> ➤ Ask yourself: *What's my anchor right now?*
>   → A thought, fear, excuse, or external attachment.
> ➤ Visualize yourself gently untying it.
> ➤ Write this down:
>   *"I bless what kept me safe. And I release it to move*
>   *forward."*

Because you weren't made for the harbor.
You were made for the **horizon**.

CAPSULE 45

Prometheus and the Fire

"Some gifts are so powerful; they must be stolen from the gods."

In the time before time, humans lived in cold darkness.
No warmth.
No light.
No spark.

The gods kept **fire** for themselves—
a symbol of power, knowledge, and transformation.

But one Titan—**Prometheus**—couldn't stand to watch humanity suffer.
He believed we were meant for more.
So one night, he **stole the fire** from Mount Olympus.
Smuggled it in a fennel stalk.
And brought it down to earth.

Flames flickered for the first time in human hands.
Light filled the caves.
Food was cooked.
Tools were forged.
Civilization began.

But Prometheus paid a price.

Zeus chained him to a rock—
where an eagle tore at his liver each day, only for it to grow back at night.

An eternal punishment...
for igniting a future that wasn't supposed to exist.

But even as he suffered,
Prometheus **never regretted giving the gift**.

Because to **elevate others**,
sometimes, you must be willing to endure.

The Flame Within

Every generation has its Prometheus.
The one who sees what could be, not just what is.
The one who rebels—not for ego, but for evolution.

- ➤ Teachers who break the rules to awaken a child
- ➤ Inventors who risk failure to offer a breakthrough
- ➤ Writers who tell the truth when silence feels safer
- ➤ You, when you choose the harder path because it's the one that matters

The world is still full of locked gates and stolen light.
Still full of people stuck in the cold.

And maybe you are the one meant to bring the fire.

Not everyone will understand.
Not everyone will thank you.
But history is changed by those who dare to strike the match.

Daily Action:

Ask yourself: *What "fire" do I hold that the world needs?*
→ An idea? A talent? A voice? A belief?

Write this:
"Even if it burns me, I will carry the flame."

Take one bold action today to share, speak, teach, or build—despite the risk.

Because some of the greatest acts in history weren't safe.
But they were **sacred**.

Stopping by Woods on a Snowy Evening

"Stopping by Woods on a Snowy Evening" By
Robert Frost

Whose woods these are I think I know.
His house is in the village though;
He will not see me stopping here
To watch his woods fill up with snow.

My little horse must think it queer
To stop without a farmhouse near
Between the woods and frozen lake
The darkest evening of the year.

He gives his harness bells a shake
To ask if there is some mistake.
The only other sound's the sweep
Of easy wind and downy flake.

The woods are lovely, dark and deep,
But I have promises to keep,
And miles to go before I sleep,
And miles to go before I sleep.

<u>End</u>